writing guides

Realistic STORIES

STORIES THAT RAISE ISSUES

SYLVIA CLEMENTS

PHOTOCOPIABLE PHOTOCOPIABLE PHOTOC

FICTION FOR AGES 7-9

CONTENTS

INTRODUCTION

The Scholastic *Writing Guides* series provides teachers with ideas and projects that promote a range of writing, bringing insights from educational research into the classroom. Each guide explores a different type of writing and provides example material, background information, photocopiable activities and teaching suggestions. Their aim is to enable teachers to guide the writing process, share planning ideas and develop themes as a context for writing activities.

The materials:

- motivate children with interesting activities
- break complex types of writing into manageable teaching units
- focus on and develop the typical features of particular types of writing
- provide original approaches to teaching.

Each book is divided into sections, beginning with examples of the type of writing being taught. These are followed by ideas for developing writing and projects that will extend over a series of sessions.

SECTION ONE: USING GOOD EXAMPLES

Section One looks at good examples of the genre, with the emphasis on using texts to stimulate and develop writing. Two example texts are shared, and questions that focus the discussion on their significant features are suggested. This is followed by activities that explore what the texts can teach us about writing, enabling teachers to compare the two texts and to go on to model the type of writing presented in the guide.

SECTION TWO: DEVELOPING WRITING

Section Two moves from reading to writing. This section provides activities that prompt and support children in planning and writing. A range of approaches includes planning templates and strategies to stimulate ideas. The activities refine children's ideas about the type of writing being developed and give them focused writing practice in the context of scaffolded tasks. Teacher's notes support each activity by explaining the objective and giving guidance on delivery.

SECTION THREE: WRITING

Section Three moves on to writing projects. Building upon the earlier work in Section Two, these projects aim to develop the quality of writing and provide a selection of ideas for class or group work on a particular theme or idea. The teacher may choose to use some or all of the ideas presented in each project as a way of weaving the strategies developed in Section Two into a more complex and extended writing task.

SECTION FOUR: REVIEW

Section Four supports the assessment process. Children are encouraged to reflect on the type of writing they are tackling and to evaluate how effectively their work has met the criteria for the genre identified in Section One.

"What's the trouble, Tommy?"

Mr Sutherland's voice droned on at the front of the class, while Tommy gazed out of the window near the back. There wasn't much to see. He turned back to the classroom, looking over the rows of desks in front of him to the blackboard, where the squiggles made no more sense than usual. Tommy knew he should concentrate, but he couldn't. He stared at the long line of marks on the top of his jotter – one for each day his dad had been gone – and sadly added another.

"Remembrance Day began after the First World War." Mr Sutherland squiggled on the blackboard as he spoke. "They called it the war to end all wars, but twenty-one years later there was another one, even bigger. The Second World War. On Sunday we remember both of them. This is one of the most famous poems from the first – the Great War. I'd like you to copy it into your jotters."

Tommy grasped his pencil tight, his tongue between his teeth, and set to work as the teacher prowled about. Bent ever closer over his book, he felt Mr Sutherland approach from behind, the creeping shadow of a growling cloud.

"What's all this, Thomas Cameron?" Mr Sutherland asked, sliding the jotter off the desk. Tommy's paralysed pencil left a thick grey line on the page, like a smoke trail from a plane about to crash. Tommy stiffened: whenever a teacher used his full name, it spelt trouble. Mr Sutherland read from the board:

In Flanders fields the poppies blow
Between the crosses, row on row

And then from Tommy's jotter:

Tommy winced. Nearby classmates nudged each other into titters.

Mr Sutherland flicked back through the pages to yesterday's lesson, and beyond. "Tommy Cameron. Tommy Cameron. Tommy Cameron," he read again.

He put the jotter down with a sigh. Tommy stared hard at the desk top. "What's the trouble, Tommy? Can't write? Can't read? Or just can't be bothered?"

from *Tommy Trouble* by Stephen Potts

Explain!

Kitty always used to say she didn't want to do this or that. Then there was a change – *she* wanted to do things, but the grown-ups wouldn't let her. Instead of saying, "I don't want to!" she found herself asking, "Why not?" Very often.

One day, for example, she asked Mum if she could walk to school on her own. "No," said Mum firmly.

"Why not?"

"You know why not," smiled Mum.

"No, I don't!"

Mum thought. "Well, because you might have an accident."

"But there's a lollipop lady!"

"Anyway, you're too young."

"Lots of my friends go to school on their own. So why not me?"

"*Because.*" Mum wasn't smiling now.

"Because what?" asked Kitty.

"Because I said so," said Mum, folding her arms.

"That's not a good reason," said Kitty.

When she went to school she told William and Rosie what had happened. "Oh, my mum always says that," sighed Rosie.

"So does mine," said William.

"It's not fair," said Kitty. "Grown-ups never think they have to explain things."

"They wouldn't like it if we acted the same," said Rosie.

Just then, the bell went – but Kitty had started to think. And at play-time she told William and Rosie her plan.

"Do you both think we should be allowed to go to school on our own, instead of being treated like babies?"

"Yes," said Rosie and William.

"And do you think grown-ups should give proper *reasons*?" Kitty asked.

They agreed.

"Well here's what we do..." said Kitty.

from *Why not?* by Bel Mooney

SECTION ONE

USING GOOD EXAMPLES

Realistic stories provide the reader with situations with which they may be familiar or can relate to. The stories may focus on a variety of situations – family issues, bullying, prejudice, belonging to a group, friendships, holiday adventures, new pets, and so on. The reader of a realistic story should be able to relate to the character's feelings and actions. The story may be funny or sad, may represent hopes and dreams or may deal with solving difficult situations. Realistic stories may make the reader think, 'If that was me...' or 'If I was in that situation...'. The characters should be realistic, the settings familiar and the situations possible or probable.

The extracts featured in this section explore contrasting realistic issues. The focus in **Tommy Trouble** *is on personal sadness and difficulties, the author using powerful phrases to evoke Tommy's feelings and to help the reader picture the situation. In the second extract, the style is more light-hearted and greater emphasis is placed on dialogue to portray the issue of Kitty feeling unhappy about parental reasoning.*

During this writing project, encourage the children to read examples of the genre. This will provide a good grounding for their own writing. For example:

- **Bullies at School** *by Theresa Breslin (Canongate Books Ltd) – bullying*
- **Kamla and Kate** *by Jamila Gavin (Mammoth) – friendship*
- **The Runner** *by Keith Gray (Mammoth) – arguing parents/running away*
- **Julian, Dream Doctor** *by Ann Cameron (Yearling Books) – doing something special*
- **Dolphin Boy** *by Julie Bertagna (Mammoth) – siblings/disabilities.*

Shared activities

"What's the trouble, Tommy?"

The extract on photocopiable page 4 features Tommy, a boy who has several issues going on in his life – his father is absent, he struggles with school work and his teacher is unsympathetic to his difficulties. World War I provides a 'backdrop'.

Display the extract on an OHP (or use an enlarged photocopy) and read the text with the children. How do they think Tommy is feeling? Ask them which phrases tell them that he is unhappy in the class – for example, *gazed out of the window; should concentrate, but he couldn't; Tommy's paralysed pencil*. Encourage the children to explain why the author uses these phrases – what images do they see?

Focus on the way the author portrays Tommy as the teacher's prey and the teacher as the predator; highlight the verbs *prowled; stiffened, winced*. Ask the children what sort of teacher they think Mr Sutherland is. Use one colour to highlight verbs describing Tommy's actions and another for the teacher's. Look for the metaphor (*the creeping shadow of a growling cloud*) and simile (*like a smoke trail from a plane about to crash*) the author uses, and the effective short sentence, *Tommy stared hard at the desk top*. Discuss how these add to the sense of his fear and despair.

Explain!

Bel Mooney's series of books featuring Kitty were inspired by her own little girl and explore issues experienced by all children, whatever their situation. In the extract on photocopiable page 5, Kitty questions a decision made by her mother and, dissatisfied with her reasoning, plots with her peers to find a way around her mother's decision. In contrast to the first extract in which the main character is a victim, this character is empowered.

Display the extract on an OHP (or use an enlarged photocopy) and read the text together. Ask the children what the 'issue' is. Essentially the issue is about independence and Kitty growing up faster than her parents will allow. Ask the children to find the reasons that Mum gives Kitty for her decision. What final reason makes Kitty annoyed and unhappy with her mother's decision? (*'Because I said so'*).

Encourage the children to give examples of when their parents have said, 'Because I said so!' Can they recall their feelings and actions? What was Kitty's reaction to her mother's decision? (She asked her friends for their opinions and decided to take action with their support.) The author raises the issue through the use of dialogue.

Tommy's trouble

The activity on photocopiable page 8 encourages children to look back at the text to find evidence to support what they have assumed about the main character Tommy. Put the children into pairs to find and highlight the phrases that support the character statements, using a copy of the extract on photocopiable page 4. They can then use photocopiable page 8 to record where the evidence was found in the extract. Encourage more able children to write the supporting phrases on the photocopiable sheet in small writing near to the boxes. Discuss the children's findings.

Why not?

Discuss the main issue in the extract on photocopiable page 5, encouraging the children to identify the two strands – Kitty is not allowed to walk to school alone and she is unhappy to accept the decision because she is not satisfied with the explanations her mother gives. Can the children identify the first two reasons offered (she might have an accident; she is too young) and the third ('Because I said so')?

Ask the children to discuss in pairs other reasons that Kitty's mother could have given for her decision and the response they think Kitty would give, bearing in mind Kitty has an answer for everything! Record some of the children's ideas. Children should then complete photocopiable page 9. Choose one of the finished pieces of work to demonstrate the story writing process, showing the class how to convert ideas into a piece of narrative.

Stories that raise issues

The extracts on photocopiable pages 4 and 5 contrast strongly with each other but are both based on the realistic story writing structure. Both extracts feature a *problem* encountered by a main character, the problem involves a *conflict* with a second character, which results in a *climax* of action and finally a *resolution* to the problem. Other characters may be involved in supporting the main character (in Kitty's case, it is her friends William and Rosie).

Use photocopiable page 10 with the children to elicit how the stories are structured. The extracts demonstrate the problem and the conflict. Discuss what may happen in the climax and resolution in both stories. For the climax, perhaps Tommy will run away from home in search of his father; Kitty may decide to go to school alone and get lost. Finally, decide on the resolution to each extract – does Tommy's father come home and help him with his school work? Maybe Kitty gets so scared that she comes to understand her mother's decision. Ask the children to complete photocopiable page 10. If the books are available (*Tommy Trouble* by Stephen Potts and *Why not?* by Bel Mooney, both published by Mammoth), the children's ideas can be compared with the original versions.

Realistic story writing

The questions on photocopiable page 11 prompt the children to consider what they have already learned through carrying out the Section One activities and will remind them to address each question as they create their own realistic stories.

Tommy's trouble

We can tell a lot about Tommy from this extract. The mind map below shows what we know. Find evidence in the extract to support these statements. Write the line number in the box to show where you found the evidence.

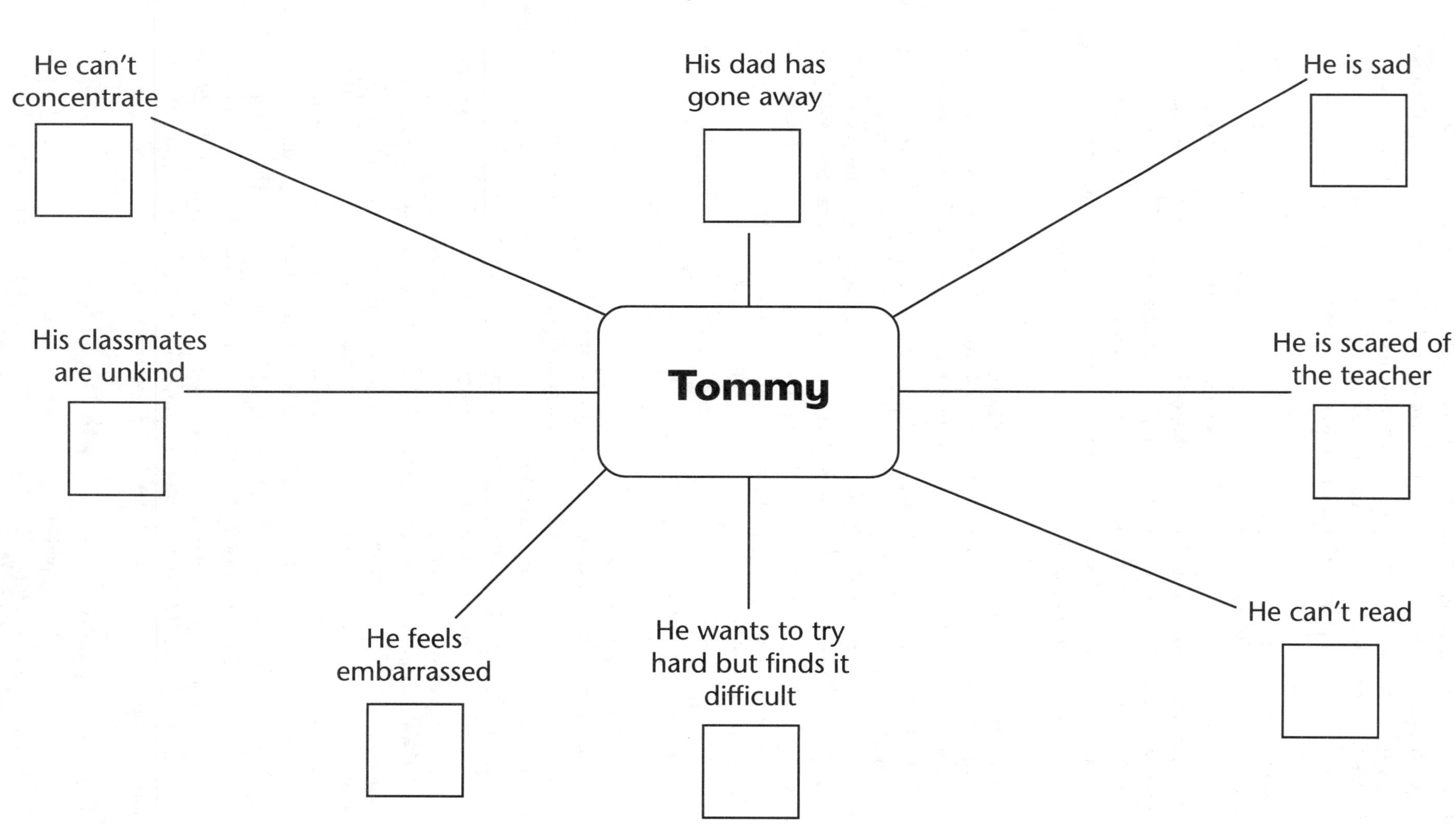

Why not?

The issue in this story is that Kitty is not allowed to walk to school on her own. Kitty doesn't think her mum gives her a good enough reason why she can't. In the speech bubbles write your own reason Kitty's mum might give and Kitty's response. In the boxes explain what they are feeling.

Stories that raise issues

Stories that raise issues have a clear structure. The extracts introduce the problem and who the conflict is between, but can you decide what happens and how the story ends?

Tommy Trouble

The problem:

The conflict:

The climax:

The resolution:

Explain!

The problem:

The conflict:

The climax:

The resolution:

Realistic story writing

SECTION TWO
DEVELOPING IDEAS

Section 2 provides activities which prompt children to expand and develop their ideas about issues they may like to write about, develop a main character, create supporting characters, decide on and create a realistic setting and develop effective dialogue. The children will draw on their experience of this genre gained from the Section One texts, their own reading and their own experience of different issues.

Teacher demonstration, shared composition and drama activities are crucial at this stage to enable children to develop their own style and to write in role as the main character. Providing opportunities for children to read their own work aloud plays an important part in the development of a written style. Activities are also included, therefore, which offer opportunities for supported composition in which children can develop specific aspects of their written style, read out their work to either the class or a writing response partner, and consider its effectiveness in respect of realistic story writing.

THINK ABOUT THE ISSUES

OBJECTIVE

■ To consider a range of potential issues.

WHAT YOU NEED

Circle time prompt cards (photocopiable page 17, enlarged onto card and cut up), photocopiable page 18, object (a teddy bear), writing materials.

WHAT TO DO

Ask the children to sit in a circle, and place the cards face down in the centre. Recap on the issue Kitty faced in the extract on photocopiable page 5. Tell the children they are going to use the cards to think about issues they could write about, drawing on their own experiences. Use a teddy bear or similar object to set circle time rules: only the child holding the bear can speak – the others listen. When another child wishes to speak, the bear is passed to them; it is then their turn. This develops listening skills and does not put individuals on the spot.

Select a child to pick a card and read it out. Pass the bear to a child who wishes to contribute a time when they experienced saying what is on the card. For example, prompt the children to relate the problem, conflict, climax and resolution, so that they can see how their experiences are stories in themselves.

After the circle time activity the children should use the discussions as a stimulus to complete photocopiable page 18. Encourage them to add extra ideas that they may not have had time to contribute.

DEVELOPING THE ISSUE

OBJECTIVE

■ To choose an issue and to consider how it can be developed into a story.

WHAT YOU NEED

Completed photocopiable page 18, photocopiable page 19, board or flip chart, individual whiteboards or notebooks, writing materials.

WHAT TO DO

Now the children have a list of issues, compiled in the previous activity, encourage them to choose one for their own story and to develop the issue into a loose story structure. (They are *not* planning their stories at this stage.) Children can work in writing pairs to enable them to bounce ideas off each other, or work alone if they choose. They should jot down their ideas on whiteboards or in notebooks. Explain that the issue will involve a main character, a supporting character or confidant(e) – this may be a toy or pet rather than a person – and someone with whom there is a conflict.

Allow plenty of time for the children to talk to the class about their work, as this verbalisation develops clarity of ideas and highlights potential stumbling blocks. It will enable the children to hear how their ideas sound and will develop editing skills. Draw an 'issue flow chart' on the board with subheaded boxes as follows:

PROBLEM ⇨ CONFLICT ⇨ CLIMAX ⇨ RESOLUTION

Tell the children to copy this flow chart and use it to outline their story before completing photocopiable page 19.

CREATING A CHARACTER

WHAT YOU NEED

Completed photocopiable page 19, photocopiable page 20 (enlarged, and one copy for each child), drawing or photograph of a boy or girl, board or flip chart, writing materials.

OBJECTIVE

- To create a character in relation to the problem he or she faces.

WHAT TO DO

The children should all now have an outline of an issue they are going to use for their own stories in Section Three. Explain that they are also going to help you to write a class story over a number of lessons. Once the children have established their *own* story plans, show them your completed copy of photocopiable page 19 and issue flow chart (see previous activity) for an issue which you consider suitable for development with your class.

Tell the children what *your* issue is going to be about (bullying, moving house, the dentist and so on). Once you have outlined your story plan and discussed your completed copy of photocopiable 19, explain that you need to develop a character who will experience the issue. For example, if your issue is about the fears of moving house and starting a new school, what sort of character would find this difficult – would it be someone who is shy and frightened of making new friends?

Display the picture of the boy or girl on the board. Explain that this is your main character but that we know nothing about him or her at present. Talk about the issue to encourage the children to think about who the character is. Supplement the picture with a name, the character's feelings, thoughts, details of interests or hobbies, and so on. Decide on characteristics such as shyness, stubbornness – whatever is relevant to the issue the character is facing. Fill in an enlarged copy of photocopiable page 20.

The children can then, in the same session or in a further session, use photocopiable 20 to develop their own main character (using their own issue flow chart and their completed copy of photocopiable 19). The central box can be used for a drawing of their character.

YOUR CHARACTER'S FEELINGS AND ACTIONS

WHAT YOU NEED

Completed photocopiable pages 19 and 20 (teacher's version and children's versions), photocopiable page 21.

OBJECTIVE

- To develop the character (and issue) by considering how his or her feelings change.

WHAT TO DO

Explain to the children that the character's feelings will change through the story as the issue progresses to a resolution. If we take the issue of moving house – to begin with, the child may be frightened and unhappy, then nervous when starting the new school, but by the resolution, he or she may find confidence, be pleased and excited. Display your copy of photocopiable page 20 from the previous activity and complete photocopiable 21 for the teacher's/class story. If the issue was about moving house, for the 'problem' section, ask the children how your character would be feeling as he or she is getting ready to move – what could your character be doing that would portray these feelings to the reader? For example: she is feeling sad and reflective; she is packing her things slowly, gazing sadly at school photographs; small objects remind her of happy times she has had with her friends.

Then move onto the 'climax' section. For the issue of moving house, perhaps the climax comes on the first day of starting the new school – the character is scared and nervous; she usually has a big appetite at breakfast but today cannot swallow because her stomach is twisting and turning; she is very quiet and drags her feet as she gets in the car to go to school.

For the 'resolution' you may decide on a happy ending – the character is now happy and excited about a new friend – perhaps she writes a letter to her old friends to tell them all about all the exciting things she is looking forward to.

Once you have demonstrated completion of photocopiable 21, the children can complete their own copies, using their notes on photocopiable pages 19 and 20 for support.

SUPPORTING AND CONFLICTING CHARACTERS

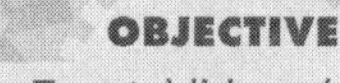

OBJECTIVE

- To establish and clarify the roles of other characters in the story.

WHAT YOU NEED

Photocopiable page 20 (completed teacher's enlarged copy and further A4 blank copies), writing materials.

WHAT TO DO

Refer to the extracts studied in Section One (photocopiable pages 4 and 5) to elicit who the other characters were and the role they played in the stories – Tommy's teacher and peers, Kitty's mother and her friends. Use the character you have created in class and the issue you have outlined as a class to discuss who else might play a role in the story. Create two other characters for the class story – one who is in conflict with the main character and one who supports the main character. For example, with the issue of moving house the supporting character may be a friend who the main character is leaving behind, or a teddy bear who the main character talks to about his or her feelings. The conflicting character may be the father who has a new job and does not find the time to consider his child's worries.

Put the children into groups of three, each taking on one of the roles in the class story (for example, the main character, the friend who is left behind and the father). Allow time for role-play in order to develop action and dialogue which may take place at the first two stages of the story – the problem and the climax.

Begin with the problem. Set the scene: for example, the father has asked the child (the main character) to help with the packing; the child is packing her things and talking to her friend who has come round to help and to say goodbye. Let the children role-play the scene, while you circulate and support this activity until you are satisfied that the children have established a role for each character. Then choose a group who performed well and explain that you are going to interview each of the characters to question their actions, assess their feelings and elicit more facts about the situation. Guide your interview to clarify the characters' roles. Follow with other groups who are willing to participate.

Now role-play the climax of the story – for moving house this may be the morning of the first day at the new school with the main character and the father at breakfast.

This role-play session can now be used to allow the children to create their own supporting characters using further copies of photocopiable 20.

DIALOGUE IN STORIES

OBJECTIVE

■ To develop characterisation through dialogue.

WHAT YOU NEED

Photocopiable pages 4 (enlarged), 21 (completed teacher's version) and 22, board or flip chart, writing materials.

WHAT TO DO

Stories about issues rely on the characters to steer the plot by what they say and do. What the characters say, how they say it and how they behave will reveal their personalities without the need for long character descriptions. This advanced narrative skill must be demonstrated to young writers through reading lots of examples and through teacher modelling. Display the last three paragraphs of 'What's the trouble, Tommy?' on photocopiable page 4. Ask the children what is happening and how Tommy is feeling. Demonstrate that Tommy's actions reveal that he is scared and embarrassed without actually saying so and that the dialogue suggests that the teacher is bullying him.

Use other examples which demonstrate dialogue interspersed with descriptions of actions that reveal feelings. Provide the children with a scenario from the problem stage of the class story for which you can build up a piece of dialogue. Establish how the characters are feeling, what they might do to show this, and what they may say. (The completed class copy of photocopiable page 21 will provide a starting point for this.) Demonstrate how to complete the first part of photocopiable page 22, then use it to model writing a piece of dialogue. Use verbs other than *said*, use adverbs, vary sentence length to create impact, include descriptive detail.

An example of dialogue in the moving house scenario may develop from photocopiable page 22 as follows:

> Amy stared down into her cereal bowl and stirred the milk aimlessly.
> 'Eat your breakfast, we're in a hurry,' her father said sternly.
> 'I'm not really hungry,' muttered Amy without looking up. A big tear rolled down her cheek and plopped into the soggy Chocco-Pops.

DEVELOP A SETTING

OBJECTIVE

■ To create a realistic setting in time and place.

WHAT YOU NEED

Objects or pictures for use as prompts, board or flip chart, whiteboards or notebooks, writing materials.

WHAT TO DO

The setting is important to create atmosphere in a story and the use of detail can bring the setting to life. Consideration of the passing of time and the weather can be used to evoke and support the feelings and actions of the characters. Consideration of objects or furniture which may be in the setting is also useful as these can act as props to support actions and feelings. For example, in *Tommy Trouble* certain features of a classroom are used to develop the issue – the window, rows of desks, Tommy's jotter, Tommy's desk. Ask the children how these features of a setting are used to create atmosphere.

Decide on a setting for the class story and present the children with a suitable object or picture which may be found in that setting. Ask them how this may feature

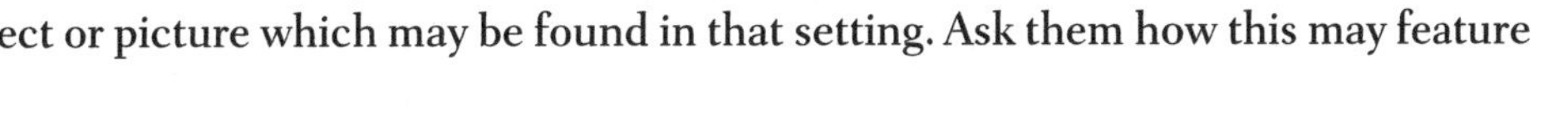

in the story to develop atmosphere about the issue. For example, if your story is about bullying, a bell could be used: the school bell ringing for playtime could trigger fear in the main character. Demonstrate how to write a few sentences incorporating a feature of the setting. For example:

> The bell rang for playtime. For most, this signalled freedom but for Amy it was like the bell at the start of a round of boxing. Fear welled up inside her, her stomach tied itself in knots as, reluctantly, she gathered up her books.

Put the children into groups of three or four and provide each group with an object or picture. Ask them to discuss and produce two or three sentences on a whiteboard for the class issue, which incorporate their object. They should consider what the character does with the object, and how the object helps to develop the issue.

Invite the groups to share their work, highlighting good examples and improving others. Children can then go on to decide on their own setting and make a list of objects they would include in their stories.

STORY OPENINGS

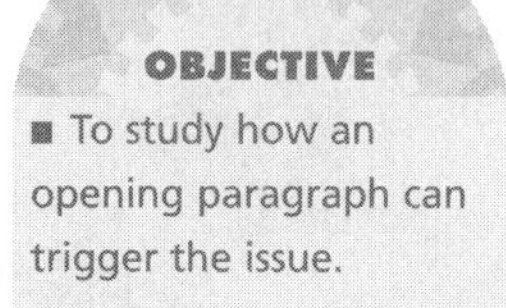

OBJECTIVE

■ To study how an opening paragraph can trigger the issue.

WHAT YOU NEED

Photocopiable page 23 (cut up into individual extracts), other extracts from stories which introduce the issue and main character in the opening paragraph – for example, *Kamla and Kate* by Jamila Gavin (Mammoth), *The Diddakoi* by Rumer Godden (Pan Books), *The Runner* by Keith Gray (Mammoth). (Ensure a mixture of first- and third-person narratives.)

WHAT TO DO

Provide the children with different opening paragraphs from your selection and ask them to read them aloud. Discuss what we find out and how the author has introduced the issue and the main character. Find the trigger points which initiate action in the scene. Identify whether stories are written in the first or third person.

Elicit the following points when discussing the four opening paragraphs from the photocopiable sheet:

Title:	Red Eyes at Night	Loudmouth Louis	Bullies at School	The Fly-by-Night
Issue:	Unwanted responsibility	Being left out/ talking in class	Bullying	New school
Narrative:	First person	First person	Third person	Third person
Issue trigger:	And who has to look after her?	It was my own fault, I admit.	'SPECKY-WECKY FOUR-EYES! WECKY-SPECKY FOUR-EYES!'	The only thing Biddy didn't like in the new town was her new school.
Style:	Use of a question	Confession to something – not yet stated!	Direct speech	Description of the school

Ask the children to refer to all the work they have completed so far (photocopiable pages 19–22) and draft their own opening paragraph. Provide them with trigger points to use to initiate the issue such as *Everything was fine until one day… All of a sudden… It wasn't until…*

They may wish to use some of the techniques outlined above, such as questions, direct speech, time phrases and so on. For a child who needs more support, use his or her story outline to help model an opening paragraph, in order to demonstrate different writing techniques.

Think about the issues

Say more about the issues

Write about the issues you could use in a story.

Developing the issue

Write your chosen issue in the centre. Now use the surrounding boxes to carefully note ideas for the structure of your story.

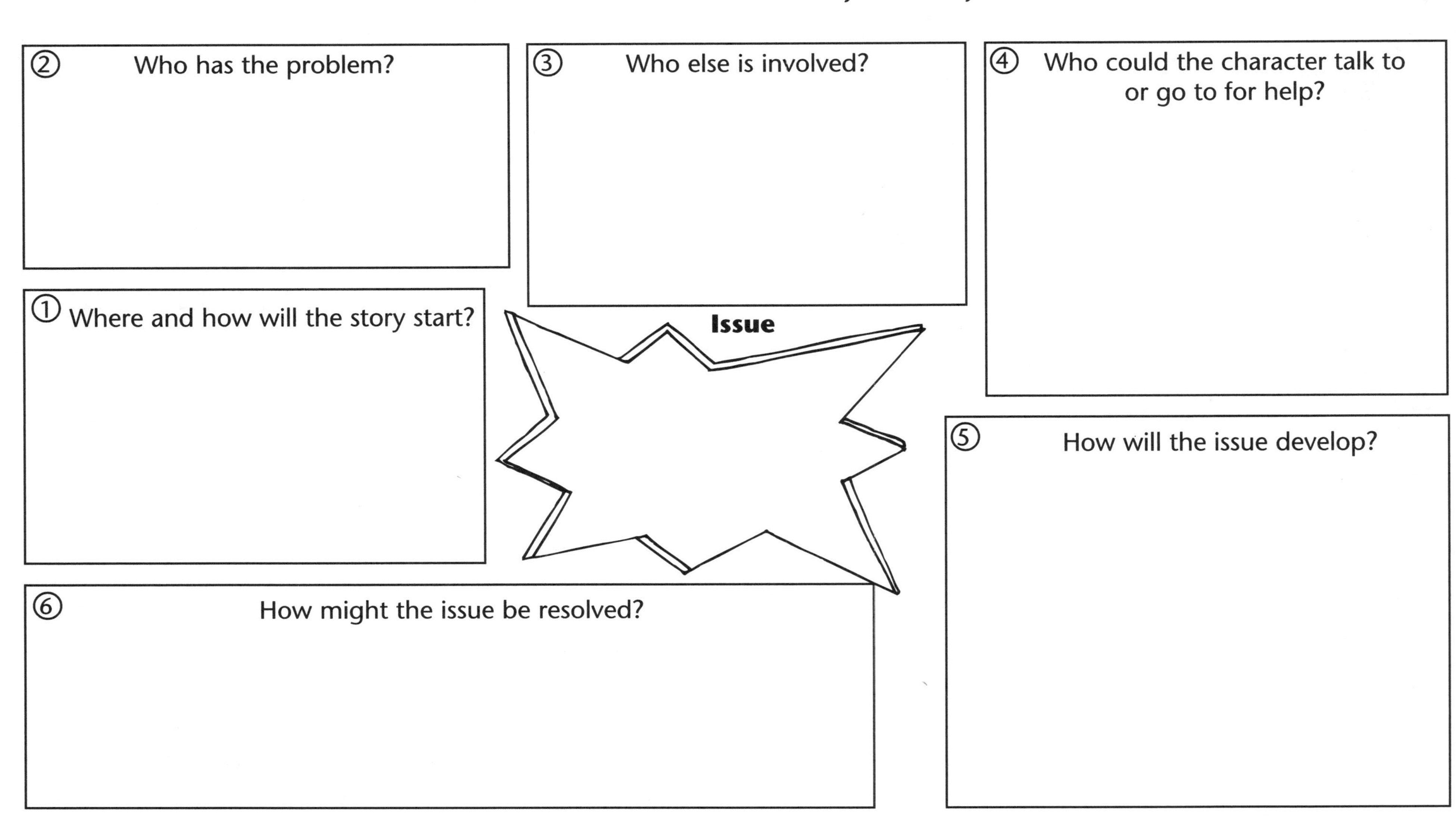

Creating a character

Name:

Family:

Appearance:

Characteristics:

Hobbies:

Best friend:

Your character's feelings and actions

Character's name: ______________________

Age: ________

Character's problem: ______________________

____

____

The problem stage

Feeling	What will he/she do to show this?

The climax stage

Feeling	What will he/she do to show this?

The resolution stage

Feeling	What will he/she do to show this?

Dialogue in stories

Character 1:	Character 2:
Feeling:	Feeling:

1.

2.

Now write this as a piece of dialogue with description. Don't forget to use speech marks!

Story openings

Red Eyes at Night

By Michael Morpurgo

My cousin Geraldine is a real little toad. Every summer holidays it's the same – Geraldine comes to stay. And who has to look after her? I do, because there's no-one else.

Loudmouth Louis

By Anne Fine

It was my own fault, I admit.

I could have been in the group that chose to organise the Raffle. But I was too busy chatting to bother to put up my hand.

And I could have joined the group Miss Sparkes said could run the Bring-And-Buy Stall. But I was leaning across to whisper something to George, so I missed that chance too.

Bullies at School

By Theresa Breslin

"SPECKY-WECKY FOUR-EYES! WECKY-SPECKY FOUR EYES!"

Siobhan Cunningham hitched her school rucksack further up her back and started to move more slowly along the road. She could now see the group at the school gate who were doing all the shouting, Karen Williams and her friends, Lyn, Rosie, Benny and Peter. They usually hung about there every morning, waiting for someone to pick on, and the someone was usually her.

The Fly-by-Night

By Saviour Pirotta

When Biddy Beck was eight, she and her mum moved from the country to a flat in a large town. Biddy liked her new home, high up in a tower block. She loved her bedroom with its green carpet, and she liked to look down on the conker trees below.

The only thing Biddy didn't like in the new town was her new school. It was huge and dark. There was a high wall round the playground. Worst of all, the children in it looked tough and unfriendly.

Section Three brings together what the children have learned about realistic story writing from Section One and uses the work they have done in Section Two to write their own realistic stories. At this stage they should have an idea of the issue they want to make into a story, a main character, supporting characters, details they wish to include to illustrate the story setting, and an opening paragraph.

The children will write their extended stories in chapters, each with a title, based on a clearly defined story plan to ensure the story has a clear structure and sense of direction. It is important to provide the right conditions for extended story writing – children should have plenty of time for planning, thinking, writing and editing. The work should also be celebrated, as this type of writing is demanding and presents a real challenge for many children. To do this, the children should be able to 'publish' their stories, making them into books which perhaps could be put in the library or given to other classes to read. This will create a real audience and give the children a sense of purpose when carrying out their writing.

Are you ready to write?

Before writing commences, the children need to formulate their ideas into a clear structure and bring together everything they have learned so far. Ensure they have a folder of all their completed work to date. Use photocopiable page 25 as a checklist to show them that now they have all the ingredients, they are ready to start cooking up their story! This checklist also provides less confident children with an opportunity to highlight areas they are unsure about. Go through each question on the sheet and locate the children's ideas from the work already completed. Ask them to circle the word *Yes* for each question once they have got a positive answer, and to jot down brief notes in the box below it.

Chapter chart

Provide the children with copies of photocopiable pages 26–8. They may like to use their opening paragraph, written during the Section Two activities, to get started on ideas for Chapter 1. They should complete each chapter plan to ensure that their story sticks to the realistic story structure and does not drift off in other directions. Check these with the children or allow them to discuss each chapter with a writing partner. Remind them that each chapter has to have a clear purpose. Once this purpose has been achieved, they can move on to the next stage of the story.

Write with style

When their plans have been prepared and checked, the children are ready to begin writing. Hand out and discuss a copy of photocopiable page 29 which provides ideas for making their writing more effective.

Remind the children to write one chapter at a time. This will result in four chapters which can be checked and edited individually. By writing in individual chapters, you will have the opportunity to mark the story in stages and provide guidance on making improvements as their story progresses. The final versions can then be assembled into a book format. To provide motivation, and help clarify events, the children can create an illustration for each chapter.

Cover it!

Once the children's stories have been completed, they can create a cover (including an illustration, title, author, price, back cover blurb, ISBN and publisher's logo). Provide them with a selection of books to help them with this process.

Are you ready to write?

Are you clear about the issue you are going to write about? **Yes No**

Do you know who your main character is? **Yes No**

Do you know who your supporting characters are? **Yes No**

Do you know where your setting will be? **Yes No**

Have you decided what setting details you will use? **Yes No**

Have you decided how you will get your story started? **Yes No**

Do you know how the story will reach a climax? **Yes No**

Do you know how your story will end? **Yes No**

Have you decided whether you will write in the first or third person? **Yes No**

Do you have a title for your story? **Yes No**

Chapter chart 1

Chapter 1 – the problem

This will:

- ★ introduce the character – what are they doing and thinking? Are they speaking to anyone? Who are they speaking to?
- ★ place the character in a setting – where are they? Will you use any setting props?
- ★ include a trigger point to introduce your issue.

Chapter title:

My notes:

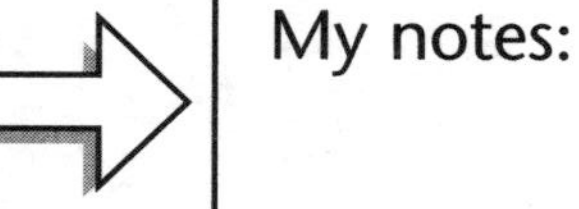

Chapter 2 – the conflict

This will:

- ★ highlight the issue by describing the main character's feelings. This may be through actions or dialogue with another character.

Chapter title:

My notes:

Chapter chart 2

Chapter 3 – the climax

This will:

★ include the main action – what happens to the main character?
★ involve a change of emotions – how is the main character feeling at this point in the story? How are you going to show this?
★ possibly involve a change of setting and a passage of time. How will you show this?

Remember: the climax is the main part of the story where a lot of the important action takes place – keep it focused and get ready to draw it to a resolution in the last chapter!

Chapter title:

My notes:

Chapter chart 3

Chapter 4 – the resolution

This will:
- ★ bring the story to a neat ending – how will you end your story?
- ★ involve a further change of emotion – have any lessons been learned by the main character as a result of the events in the story?

Chapter title:

My notes:

Illustration plan

Note down or sketch out some ideas for illustrations here:

Chapter 1	Chapter 2
Chapter 3	Chapter 4

Write with style

Use effective speech words:
sighed, muttered, shouted, mumbled, explained

Use a mixture of long and short sentences for effect and turn sentences into exclamations:
Amy gasped!
The rain beat steadily on the window. Amy gazed outside. She felt as gloomy as the weather.

When your character is thinking, use questions to illustrate his or her thoughts:
"Will I ever be happy again?" wondered Amy sadly to herself.

Use dialogue effectively, incorporating action to show how the character is feeling:
"I'm not going!" Amy shouted, stamping her foot and slamming her bag on the floor. "It's just not fair!" She burst into tears and collapsed in a heap on the bed.

Use adjectives and adverbs – but don't overuse!
Amy turned and sadly waved goodbye. She dragged her heavy school bag along the floor as she slowly made her way home.

Use time phrases to progress the story – but be realistic:
It wasn't long before...
Soon, the time had come to...
The following morning...
After what seemed like hours...

SECTION FOUR
REVIEW

Section Four provides materials to facilitate assessment and review of the children's realistic stories. The children are encouraged to look critically at their work and check that they have incorporated the features of realistic story writing covered in Sections One, Two and Three.

It is helpful to use review partners who can offer feedback, or set up editorial groups to assess individual stories. It is important to make the review process positive and find good points about every child's work to ensure that they will be motivated towards creative writing in future lessons. Children will enjoy the process if their work is valued. By creating a fictitious publishing company and giving children roles on an editorial panel with a goal to achieve, such as publishing their books for children in different classes or recording their stories for radio broadcast, they will undoubtedly be more motivated during the review process.

During the review and assessment process for realistic story writing there are key features which the children should be looking to identify in their stories:

- ***a clear issue which forms a plot based on problem – conflict – climax – resolution***
- ***a realistic, familiar setting***
- ***credible characters who have distinct roles to play in the story – empathetic main character, conflicting character, confidant(e)***
- ***trigger points which initiate or develop the problem, cause changes in emotion and help lead the story through the issue to its resolution***
- ***effective use of dialogue which helps to develop the storyline.***

Editorial review

For the review process, put the class into mixed-ability groups of approximately four or five children with their completed stories. You may decide to carry out this process before 'publishing' the final draft (to allow for amendments) or after the completed story has been published, complete with its own cover and illustrations.

Inform the children that they are to look for positive points in every story and that if they find areas which could be improved they should comment in a tactful way, for example *I like the way you… but I think this part could be improved if you…* Negative comments could be hurtful and could damage an individual's confidence.

Hand out a copy of photocopiable page 31 to each group's 'Chief Editor' for completion, using the group's comments, after the story has been heard. Explain what features they will be listening out for while hearing the stories. The more able reader in each group should then read aloud each story while the others listen and formulate their opinions. This may take several sessions to complete but the process should be valued and time given to ensure everyone's work is reviewed.

Each group could nominate one of the stories that they particularly liked and which provided the best example of realistic story writing. These stories can then be listened to by the whole class on future occasions.

Can it get any better?

The children should also be given the opportunity to review their own work. This may be an ideal homework task which they could share with parents or complete on their own. Photocopiable page 32 guides the children to look at specific areas of their story writing and to comment on how they could improve their story. Encourage the children to refer to the feature bank, incorporating the different elements in their answers.

Editorial review

Review panel: ____

____

Story title: ____

Author: ____

1.	Is the issue the main character faces clear?	Yes/No
2.	Do you feel like you know and understand the main character?	Yes/No
3.	Is there a conflict in the story?	Yes/No
4.	Does the story have a setting which you can imagine?	Yes/No
5.	Does the author use dialogue to help the storyline?	Yes/No
6.	Does the story have an exciting climax?	Yes/No
7.	Were you happy with the resolutions to the story?	Yes/No

If you have answered **No** to any of the above questions, give suggestions for how you would improve this area of the story:

List three things which you thought were good about this story (parts of the plot/effective adjectives or adverbs/trigger points, and so on):

1.

2.

3.

Can it get any better?

I think I did these things well:

I think I could have improved these things:

Feature bank

use of time phrases
use of chapters
use of exclamations
use of questions

creating a main character
using objects to help the action
creating an exciting climax
creating a satisfying resolution

use of trigger points
description of setting
use of dialogue
introduction of the problem

This is the main change I would make to improve my story: